The Complete Guide
to Petoskey Stones

The Complete Guide to Petoskey Stones

Bruce Mueller

and

William H. Wilde

The University of Michigan Press
Ann Arbor

Petoskey Publishing Company
Traverse City

Copyright © Bruce Mueller and William H. Wilde 2004
All rights reserved
Published in the United States of America by
The University of Michigan Press
and
The Petoskey Publishing Company
Manufactured in Canada
⊗ Printed on acid-free paper

2011   2010   2009   2008   7   6   5   4

ISBN 0-472-03028-0

Library of Congress Cataloging-in-Publication Data on File

Cover photograph © by Ken Scott

ISBN 978-0-472-03028-6

Introduction

"a man never stands so tall as when he stoops down to help a child"
—Bobby Jones

It is a memory that so many of us have, looking for Petoskey stones along the shores of beautiful Lake Michigan. For me, it was at the old Kay-n-Ray's Resort near Elk Rapids when I was seven years old, my mom taking me along to hunt for hours at a time.

When I had children of my own, I wanted to take them to find Petoskeys. I wanted to share with them everything I knew about Michigan's state stone—which, it turns out, is actually fossilized coral. So I went on a hunt of my own.

I started to ask around as to where you could find Petoskeys so I could take my kids to these secret places. Many people said they were hard to find because so many people have taken them from the beaches. Some people told me it was illegal to take them. I was told that Michigan was the only place where you could find them.

A perfectly polished Petoskey

Were Petoskeys like oil—with a finite supply? Could they be taken from the national lakeshore?

I stopped at the C&M Rock Shop in Honor, Michigan, and met the owner, Bruce Mueller. He answered a lot of my questions, but that made me think of more. So a week later, I went back. Bruce, again, answered all my questions, so I asked how he knew so much. "I have a masters in geology from the University of Illinois and I really like rocks," he said in his quiet and gentle way. He started to tell me more about Petoskeys, and walked off to the back of the store to grab his special collection of his most prized

Petoskeys. I knew right then and there he had to be my co-author for this book.

By then, I had already found many of the great places to hunt Petoskeys, including two places where you can find Petoskey boulders—that's right, boulders—big ones! I swam right out there, trying not to get cut on zebra mussels, and looked for myself. My wife thought I was crazy, but how many people have seen Petoskey boulders? I found places that you can easily walk right to the beach, 30 feet from your parked car, where if the storms have generated enough wind and from the right direction, you can find 10-20 good Petoskeys in an hour or so. I found some places where if you can make the hike, and again, with Mother Nature cooperating, you can find baseball-sized Petoskeys like you are picking candy from your local candy store.

But this book would have been incomplete without Bruce, his expertise, and his favorite hunting spots. He has added so much valuable information on Petoskeys. I always left our meetings more excited and hardly able to wait to tell my family. Now I hope that you get as much enjoyment and information from this book as I have had working on it. I'd like to thank Bruce Mueller, from whom I've learned so much, Dr. Reed Wicander, our expert paleontologist at Central Michigan University, for his review, and all the others who shared their special places to find Petoskey stones. May you long enjoy the hunt for all stones, and especially Michigan's state stone—the Petoskey!

—William H. Wilde

How to Use This Book

After explaining the legend of where the Petoskey name comes from, this book presents the first complete story of the Petoskey stone. It will give the true facts about the stone and its origin. The second section contains the rules and regulations about gathering stones. The third section describes where to find stones throughout northern lower Michigan. The final section shows you the various ways to polish your newly found treasures.

Where did the name Petoskey come from?

According to an old Ottawa Indian legend, a descendant of French nobility named Antoine Carre visited what is now the Petoskey area and became a fur trader with the John Jacob Astor Fur Company. In time, he met and married an Ottawa (or Odawa) Indian princess. Carre became known to the Indians as *Neaatooshing*. He was eventually adopted by the tribe and made chief.

In the spring of 1787, after having spent the winter near what is now Chicago, Chief *Neaatooshing* and his royal family started home. On the way, the party camped on the banks of the Kalamazoo River. During the night, a son was born to the Chief. As the sun rose, its rays fell on the face of the new baby. Seeing the sunshine on his son's face, the Chief proclaimed, "His name shall be *Petosegay*. He shall become an important person." The translation of the name is "rising sun," "rays of dawn," or "sunbeams of promise."

True to his father's prediction, Petosegay became an important person. He was a fur trader and merchant who acquired much land and wealth. His appearance was outstanding. His skin was smooth, his eyes sharp and deeply set, and he spoke English quite well. Ultimately, he married the young daughter of Chief Pokozeegun, a great Ottawa Chief from the northern Lower Peninsula of Michigan.

In the summer of 1873, just a few years before the death of Petosegay, a city came into being on his land along the bay at Bear Creek. The site was just a field with very few buildings and very few people actually living there. The city was named Petoskey, an English adaptation of Petosegay. Thus they honored someone who gave his land, name, and the heritage of "sunbeams of promise."

Michigan's Official State Stone

In 1965, Michigan Governor George Romney signed House Bill 2297 of 1965, making the Petoskey Michigan's official state stone.

What is a Petoskey?

We must first go back 355-415 million years to the Devonian Period. Devonian is one of the eleven geologic periods that divide the last 545 million years of earth's history, based on the fossil record. The Devonian Period was about 100 million years before the dinosaurs roamed the earth, and Michigan, then positioned near the equator, was completely covered by a warm shallow sea that extended from the Gulf of Mexico through Michigan and into Canada. On the sea bottom were corals, much like the corals you find in the seas and oceans today.

Coral grow by stages. They start out their life as free-floating planulae. The planulae eventually settle on the sea floor and attach to something hard on the sea bottom

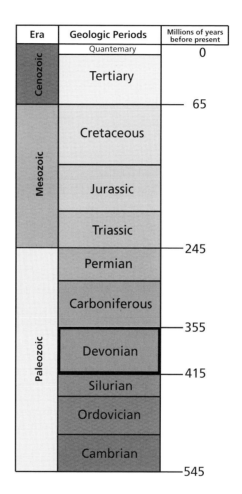

Era	Geologic Periods	Millions of years before present
Cenozoic	Quantemary	0
	Tertiary	
		65
Mesozoic	Cretaceous	
	Jurassic	
	Triassic	
		245
Paleozoic	Permian	
	Carboniferous	
		355
	Devonian	
		415
	Silurian	
	Ordovician	
	Cambrian	
		545

The Geologic Timeline

(polyp stage) where they spend the rest of their life. The coral secretes a calcite "cup like" external covering around itself called an exoskeleton. The soft-bodied coral lives within this exoskeleton and uses its tentacles to collect food.

Some corals, known as rugose corals, live solitary lives, but others are colonial (a group of many with the same characteristics). *Hexagonaria percarinatae*, the scientific name for the coral whose fossilized remains are known as

The name *Hexagonaria percarinata* (Petoskey stone) was designated by Dr. Edwin Stumm in 1969.

Petoskey stones, were colonial corals. As the polyp of *Hexagonaria* grew, it built up a six-sided cup about the size of a six-sided lead pencil. Initially, the cup is short, but in time, it may grow to the length of an ordinary lead pencil. As the polyp grows it produces buds, which become new colony members. These produce their own six-sided cups surrounding the original member of the colony. These buds in turn produce their own buds and in this way, the colony grows. As it continues budding, the colony grows upward and outward and begins, in the typical case, to look like a short-stemmed bouquet of flowers with the founding member of the colony and the early buds having the longest stem-like cups. The top of the colony creates the dome-like look of the flowers in a bouquet. Colonies can grow to one-half ton or larger. Each hexagonal (six-sided) cup is filled with a sunburst of lines that radiate away from the center. The lines, which are actually vertical partitions, are called septa (note radiating septa within the cells as shown in photo on page 13) and are there to provide support and increase the surface area for the soft body of the coral.

Eventually the coral dies. Some die of old age, some from disease, and some are eaten by predators or attacked by parasites. Some also may be buried by underwater land-slides called "turbidity currents."

When the colony dies, it is usually buried by mud, and the mud later covered by other sediments. During burial, calcium carbonate precipitates out of solution and fills in the porous areas of the coral. The mud is eventually compressed to form shale, such as the Bell Shale, Antrim Shale, and Ellsworth Shale. (If you place a small Petoskey stone in vinegar and wait overnight, the vinegar will remove the calcium carbonate that has replaced the coral and leaves a white ghost-like remnant of the original exoskeleton which is slightly more acid-resistant.)

These shales form a belt that stretches across the upper quarter of the Lower Peninsula of Michigan, beginning at Lake Huron on the eastern side of the state and going west to Lake Michigan.

Fossil corals, like *Hexagonaria*, or Petoskey stones, tell us a great deal about their environment. Corals contain algae (a one-celled organism that predominantly lives in water and contains chlorophyll and helps purify the water and air through photosynthesis) that live in their tissues.

An unusual fossil coral other than Petoskey found along Lake Michigan. Its radials are well displayed.

An example of a poorly formed Petoskey; cells that do not touch tend to be round.

The algae and corals form a symbiotic relationship, which means they both benefit from each other. The algae take carbon dioxide from the bodies of the corals and return oxygen and elements needed by the corals to live. The algae get a nice safe place to sit in the sun, which they need to live. Because of their symbiotic relation with algae, corals cannot live without sunlight, and sunlight only penetrates water well to a depth of around 200 feet. Therefore, we know that the seas covering what is now Michigan were less than 200 feet deep. Petoskeys thrived where there was an abundance of food, warm water temperatures, and sunlight.

This is how the billions and probably trillions of colonial and rugose corals lived and died in the ancient Michigan Seaway. During a long period of time, they were buried, fossilized, and later brought to the surface by the erosive forces of nature—lakes, rivers, weather, and by the building of roads and other man-made projects that expose them. In the typical case when you find a Michigan Petoskey stone, you do not have a piece of coral, you have a complete coral colony which has eroded intact from a bed of shale.

Why are Petoskeys unique?

Most corals are composed of calcium carbonate (limestone or calcite), they can be and are found in calcareous shale, and can be associated with oil. What makes Petoskeys different that is they belong to the genus *Hexagonaria*, a Devonian genus that contains many different species.

Here in Michigan the coral's porous insides were filled in by calcium carbonate, making it possible to give the stones a good polish. The corals were invaded at some time by crude oil and it is the oil that gives the stones their "soft" brown color, often with spot-like concentrations of the oil at the center of the cups. It is the amount of crude oil in a stone that determines the lightness (not much crude oil) or darkness (a lot of crude oil) of the stone's color. If you put a Petoskey stone under a black light, it will flouresce blue indicating the presence of crude oil.

An excellent example of the "oil coloration" in a Petoskey

Are Petoskeys found only in Michigan?

Most people think that Petoskeys are found only in Michigan. This is not true. They are also found in other Midwest states such as Indiana (Falls of the Ohio State Park located in Clarksville, IN—220 acres of exposed Devonian age fossil beds), Illinois, and Iowa, though certainly the highest concentrations of stones are in northwest corner of lower Michigan.

In Alaska you can find the "Alaskan Petoskey," the "Alaskan Petoskey," however, is a different genus—*Xystriphylum*.

The Alaskan "Petoskey"

The Alaskan "Petoskey" is a good example of the fact that even though they aren't really Petoskeys, you can find the same pattern of fossilized corals all around the world where *Hexagonaria* coral existed some 355-415 million years ago. However, because of calcite infilling, oil coloration, and various preservational factors, *Hexagonaria* found elsewhere are inferior to Michigan Petoskeys.

It is generally agreed that Petoskeys on the west side of the state are superior to those on the east side, or even the central part of the state, and because of the vast quantities of gravel along the shoreline of Lake Michigan, which are constantly being turned over by the pounding of the waves and winter ice, the Lake Michigan shoreline is the easiest place to hunt for them. A little known fact about Petoskeys and Michigan is that you can even find Petoskeys in the bedrock of the Upper Peninsula of Michigan, though again, your best bet is the Lake Michigan shoreline.

How to find the top of the Petoskey stone

You can find the top and bottom of a Petoskey by looking for the founding member of the colony. The top will look more evenly shaped with the six-sided design, whereas the bottom will often show a more or less centered member with other columns radiating away from it on all sides.

Glaciers and the location of Petoskeys

About 70,000 years ago, the Wisconsin Ice Sheet grew in the vicinity of Hudson Bay and moved toward Michigan. It is thought by some that this ice was about two miles thick, and eventually moved across the Lower Peninsula and carved out the basins of the Great Lakes. The glacier picked up the coral colonies that had weathered to the surface, froze to them, and incorporated them within its body, and carried them south. In the northern quarter of the state it gouged out and freed billions or trillions more from the calcareous shales in which they were entombed. As the glacier moved across the state, it left tremendous numbers of coral colonies scattered across Michigan and undoubtedly carried some into Illinois, Indiana and Iowa. When the ice melted the Petoskeys were left behind as

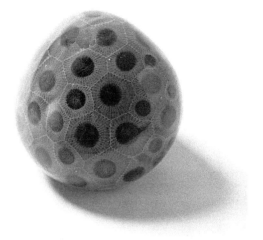

Top of a Petoskey

Bottom of a Petoskey

glacial eratics—stones carried by the glacier to places where they don't belong.

Size and shapes of Petoskeys

The glaciers, because of their enormous size and weight, were not gentle with the coral colonies they carried, and these colonies rarely have the outline of a bouquet of flowers. They are much more rounded and are likely to be covered with scratches produced as the glaciers dragged them over the bedrock. There are even examples of "smashed" Petoskeys where the nice 6-sided design is just crushed. These were smashed by the weight of overlying sediments, not by the ice.

As the waves on Lake Michigan and large northern Michigan inland lakes continue to pound their beaches,

Bouquet shape of a Petoskey

A Petoskey crushed by the enormous weight of the
overlying sediments.

the Petoskeys tend to be rounded down to the size and
shape of an oval bar of soap. Large stones, because of their
weight, have a great deal of momentum and each blow
sends a series of fractures into the stone to a depth of per-
haps an eighth of an inch. Smaller stones have much less
momentum and the fracturing barely penetrates the surface.

The shape of stones not found in or near the water are
far more irregular and less rounded. This is because they
were not subject to the tumbling action of the waves.

A dry, unpolished Petoskey

Will they ever run out?

Very few new stones are being washed out of the lake and onto the shore each year. Therefore the stones that are already on the beach are the stones that are available to collect. The gravel on the beach is constantly being turned over by the waves, which exposes new stones, but basically the stones that are there are the stones that are available to find. Fresh stones from the lake can be identified by their fuzzy appearance. They have a "rotted" look on the surface and if you sand them down you will find the cause, which is green algae growing within and below the surface of the stone. The new stones that are brought to the beach are brought in not just by waves but with the help of the

A wet, unpolished Petoskey

ice that freezes to the bottom of the lake near shore and brings stones to shore as the ice washes up in the early spring.

There are so many Petoskey stones in the northern Lower Peninsula that it is certain they will never all be collected. Were they all to be collected and put in a pile, we would have a huge pile the size of a mountain. With that said, the easy collecting of the pre-1980s is over. Take enjoyment from finding, not taking.

With this spirit, you will take solace in knowing that most of the remaining stones are not on the beaches, but rather buried in the glacial gravels or in various formations that lie below other layers of sediment.

How to determine the value of Petoskey stones

The value of a Petoskey lies in the perfection of its preservation, its color, the contrast between the color of its various parts and its size. Other things being equal, the larger the stones, the more valuable.

Rules, Regulations, and Guidelines for Picking Up Petoskeys

"Everyone should be stewards of the land."
    –Al Ammons, Leelanau State Park Ranger

Rules of the Sleeping Bear National Lakeshore

The rule for the Sleeping Bear National Lakeshore Park, is that you leave the park as you found it. The Boy Scouts have a good rule, too: leave it cleaner than you found it.

Before we get into the official rules about taking Petoskey stones, you must first know what happened to the "Green Stone" (chlorastrolite) on Isle Royal. The Green Stone is the official Michigan state gem stone. Many years ago, they were plentiful everywhere, and then people started taking them off the beaches. Now they are very hard, if not impossible in many areas to find. Let's not let this happen with the Petoskey stone.

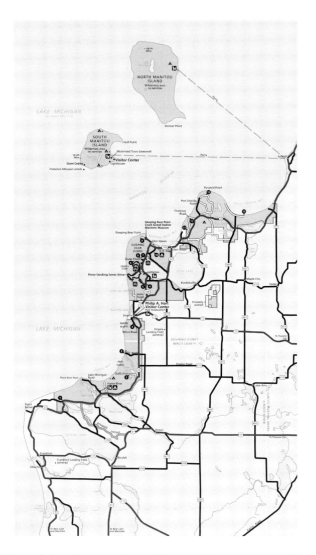

Map of the Sleeping Bear National Lakeshore, with shading showing its boundaries (Courtesy National Park Service)

The following is from Chris Johnson, Leelanau District Ranger for the National Park Service: The National Lakeshore tolerates individuals taking a stone or two for their personal viewing because of the traditional aspect of the activity, but is very strict about visitors taking quantities of stones of any type from the National Lakeshore.

They have caught people taking stones out in buckets, bags, backpacks and in truckbeds. You won't be happy if you are one of them.

The fines for taking stones out of the National Lakeshore can range from $50 to $5,000 and/or up to six months in jail. However, the high end of any fine or jail time would only be in the most extreme cases, and the ranger would base each decision on the individual case. But be forewarned, the fine for taking stones from the National Lakeshore for commercial purposes will not be light!

Michigan State Park regulations

According to Al Ammons, ranger at the Leelanau State Park, their rules are basically the same as the National Lakeshore's. Officially, their rule is you cannot destroy, damage or remove state property. This includes taking Petoskey stones from the park, though if you are only taking a few for your personal enjoyment, they won't say anything. If you are issued a ticket for taking too many Petoskeys or taking them for business reasons, you can be issued a ticket for a civil infraction and can be given a fine of not more than $500.00.

Property rights—Great Lakes

If you access the beach via a public access and want to get to a spot where you would be crossing a beach area that is private property (you will commonly see signs posted), then you need to be walking in the water to be sure you are within your rights. If you are walking between the water and the ordinary high water mark, be aware that the courts are now determining the private property line, so be safe and stay in the water. There are local customs where people do walk the beach and the owners are accommodating,

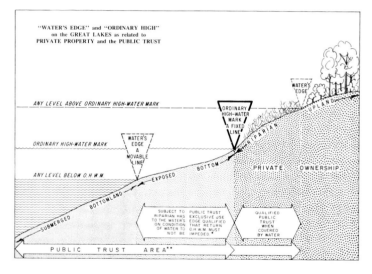

A diagram showing the water's edge and ordinary high water for the Great Lakes, so you can determine public vs. private property. (Courtesy the Leelanau Conservancy)

so make sure you are respectful of what they are allowing you to do. Be quiet, don't walk up close to their homes, leave it cleaner than you found it, and when in doubt, be conservative and stay in the water.

Property rights—inland waters

Inland waters are different than the Great Lakes. You do not have the right to walk in the water or along the shore of a private beach without permission of the property owner.

Property lines and roads

When looking for stones on the side of roads, the first rule is to make sure you get your vehicle safely to the side of the road and leave your flashers on. Be careful. Now for the property line. Typically, county road commissions and the Michigan Department of Transportation (M-DOT) have 66 feet from the center of the road. That's 33 feet from the middle to each side of the road. This can vary from road to road, so to check that you would be on public land, you should call your local road commission or the Traverse City office of M-DOT (231-941-1986). Just like walking the beaches, treat the property and property owner as you would want to be treated if you were the property owner.

Water levels and Petoskey stones

When we wrote this book, the water levels were extremely low, so finding stones in East or West Grand Traverse Bay,

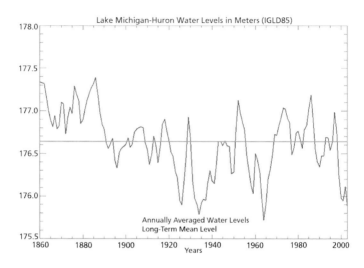

**Water levels at Lake Michigan
(Courtesy NOAA/GLERL)**

Old Mission Peninsula, the tip of the Leelanau Peninsula, and many places along Lake Michigan was much harder because algae was all over the stones. When the water levels rise, the beaches will again start to show fresh, clean stones, with no algae appearing. So watch the water levels and old places might come back as favorite spots.

Where do you find Petoskeys?

Find a beach with plenty of rocks. Sure, everybody knows that, but there are more places to look than just a beach

A polished Charlevoix stone

with stones. But before we go there, remember the rules for taking stones out of the National Lakeshore and state parks. You should also remember there are many other interesting stones to find. A great example is the Charlevoix stone, which looks fantastic when polished. There are many stones with patterns that you and your kids can make up names for. Our family has done this and we've come up with names like Saturn rocks (they have rings), Christmas rocks (green and red), and you'll have fun seeing what names you can make up! How about naming one after the kids!

Chain coral unpolished

One last thing to remember is that I've given you some nice spots, but part of the fun is to find your own spots, and without a doubt, there are many places not in this book that you can find and then share with others. Try a seasonal road, a public access, a walk down a friend's beach, or any place where there is fresh gravel (I've seen Petoskeys at the bottom of a chair lift at Crystal Mountain!). You never know where the next great spot and great experience might be found.

Beaches

Yes, of course beaches. But you want beaches that don't have moss on the rocks, and where there are large pockets

Chain coral polished

of rocks and stones, not intermittent. We will give you some nice places to look.

Cutbanks

In the nearly 40 years since I've been hunting rocks, I never thought I would find Petoskeys on the side of a road like I did the day my friend Terry showed me a cutbank. "Cutbanks" are where roads cut a path through the side of a hill, and erosion has exposed sand and rocks coming down the side. Just be careful of cars and private property. There are different laws regarding how much of the land is public property from the road, so make sure you check first.

A great beach for hunting Petoskeys is also good for picnics.

On the particular day he shared this secret with me, we found 45 nice stones in less than an hour. The best time to check a cutbank is after a day or better yet, multiple days of heavy rain, so it will reveal new stones.

Now just to make sure that Terry didn't plant these stones for my benefit (he was teasing me that he did), I did a double check. While driving along M-72, one mile west of the intersection of M-72 and County Road 675, exactly at Armstrong Road and M-72, I pulled the truck over to examine a cutbank. I couldn't believe it . . . nine stones in ten minutes, and no doubt there were many more, but it was getting dark. Once in the car, thrilled that these cut-

A classic cutbank

banks were real, I called Terry to tell him. He started laughing, knowing he had hooked me on cutbanks!

There's one more cutbank I have to share with you that is great for finding Petoskeys. From Suttons Bay, take M-204 away from the lake and on both sides of the road, one mile from the intersection of M-22 and County Road 204, is a huge cutbank. It is about 50-60 feet high and goes at least a couple of hundred feet. I found some beautiful stones here, and you can search here for quite a while.

One final point on cutbanks, the stones are a bit rougher, naturally due to the absence of the repeated wave action that smooths the stones, but I have found more of the bouquet type Petoskeys here than elsewhere.

Gravel Pits

Yes, gravel pits. Now, like cutbanks, you normally won't find the quality that you will at a good beach, but on a rainy day, you can find a nice stash of stones. Make sure you have permission from the owner before you go on the property. The best place to find gravel pits is in the Michigan Atlas & Gazetteer by DeLorme. You can find it at most bookstores, or from www.delorme.com (ISBN 0-89933-335-4). A quarry that the Geology Department at Central Michigan University sends many of its students to is located on Route 23, seven to eight miles north of Alpena. Take Rock Port Quarry Road east at the Opechee Store and proceed about three miles to an old abandoned quarry. So if you are craving a good rock hunt and you aren't near Lake Michigan, try a quarry or a gravel pit.

Fields Where Petoskeys Are

I've never found this field . . . yet. That said, I have heard from numerous sources that there is a farmer near Maple City who, when asked, has allowed people to look for stones on his property, and they find them! We are talking about right out in the middle of a farm field. This field is likely underlain by the Antrim Shale. If true, this is a sterling example that you never can tell where and when you will find your secret place. The joy is in the hunt!

Private Beaches

You have to be very careful with this one, and no doubt to try this you must really be off the chart for Petoskey stone hunting. But you can search the waters in front of private beaches, if, and only if, you can get there without setting foot anywhere on private property (remember the difference between inland lakes and the Great Lakes). Take a boat, canoe, or wade a long way. So if you belong to this elite, if not crazy group, try your luck near Cathead Point in Leelanau County, Bay Harbor in Petoskey, or any other rocky beach where there is no public access. If you are this devoted, remember to act as you would want someone to act in front of your property.

A no-trespassing sign at Christmas Cove

Seasons to find stones

The best season to hunt for stones, all other criteria being equal (post-storm) would be spring. The winter storms and ice have churned up the beach and exposed new stones. Fall is often good, too, because the sand on some beaches washes away by fall and then drifts down again during the winter and spring.

Guaranteed spots to find your Petoskeys

The first thing that you have to remember when you hunt for Petoskeys is that the guardian rule that *the hunt* itself is the best part. Finding your spot is THE best experience. Sharing it with some of your friends, who will relish your discovery the same way you did when you found it, is the next best.

With that said, I am going to give you some spots I am sure you will enjoy that have been shared with me by others. So if you need a place that has a very good chance of success, say to start a youngster on the joys of rock hunting, these are solid, solid bets.

Now, once you get to your destination, remember, no matter how many you find or don't find, relish every trip and soak up every sunset, beautiful tree or terrain, and leave every spot cleaner than you found it.

PETOSKEY & CHARLEVOIX AREA

The basic rule in this area is, anywhere you can find access to the beach can be a good area to find Petoskeys. Bring your camera, pack a picnic, and you can have a great time exploring. Below, I've listed a few that are tried and true, but can be busier, so what's to stop you from finding your own area once you've hit these?

Petoskey State Park (231-547-6641)

It is only fitting that we start with Petoskey State Park. This is the tried and true place where it all started and though it certainly is not a secret, it is still a good place to

Petoskey stone hunting with kids is a great spring, summer or fall activity.

find our official state stone. All told, it is about five miles worth of picking. Some places are better than others here for finding Petoskeys (I found heading south was better), so the further you hike to separate yourself from others looking for Petoskeys, the more stones you should find. This entire area is rich for hunting. You should also remember that this is one of the most spectacular views of the big lake you'll see.

The park is 6 miles SE of Harbor Springs, on M-119.

Fisherman's Island State Park (231-347-1027)

One mile south of Charlevoix is another spectacular place to soak up the view while hunting. If you are heading

An example of what a great find looks like from the Petoskey area

south outside of Charlevoix on US 31, take a right on Bells Bay Road, which takes you by the large CEMEX plant. Go 1.2 miles and veer left on the seasonal road and you'll see the lake! From the entrance of the park, you have 2.5 miles of road to the south. Near the park entrance are a lot of stones on the beach, and I found some good stones there, but my best luck was at the end of the 2.5 mile road. There is a stream that empties into the lake. Here I found 17 small, but perfect stones in the shallow stream. The beach itself doesn't have as many stones as it does near the park entrance.

Glenn's Market North (not South) in Petoskey

Here's another great spot that locals go to. The travel writer for Booth Newspapers wrote about it a while ago, so I had to call and check. Twice in fact, and both times the employees said "Yes. People find stones here." In back of the supermarket there is a parking area and short trail to the beach. Just go to the corner of US 31 and M-119 and it is on your left.

Magnus City Park

From the US-31 traffic light closest to downtown Petoskey, turn west on Lake Street, cross the Bear River at City Hall and follow the signs to the shore. Like so many places in and around Petoskey, this is a good, solid bet to find stones. Sunset Park is just north of here, again on US 31, and is a good spot.

Bay Harbor

East Park (South of Bay Harbor) and West Park (North of Bay Harbor) provide excellent public lake accesses next to this multi-million dollar resort. East Park is less fancy and has a parking lot 1/4 mile from the 75 stairs that take you down to the beach. East Park is less traveled and a good place to find Petoskeys. West Park has nicer facilities, two great parking lots, a play structure, and it's only 30-40 feet from the beach. Excellent for older rock hunters, ones with bad knees, and children.

Lake Michigan Shores Roadside Park

Go five miles north of Charlevoix, still on US 31, and there is a roadside park named Lake Michigan Shores. I only found two stones, but that doesn't mean you won't find more. This is a beautiful stop, and the view alone is worth it. There is another little access site ¼ mile north of this that you can hunt from as well.

Norwood

Driving south of Charlevoix on US 31, take a right on Norwood Road. Go two miles (and enjoy some nice panoramic views of the water and a nice driving road) and you come into quaint Norwood. Take a right on Lake Street, past the Norwood Township Hall, (a Michigan Historic Site) and keep going straight to the beach (it turns into a seasonal road). The road takes a right near the beach and there is a little access site. I found a lot of stones here and met a nice lady named Lynda, who hopefully I showed

The Norwood Road sign off of US 31

The great view driving down to Norwood and Lake Michigan

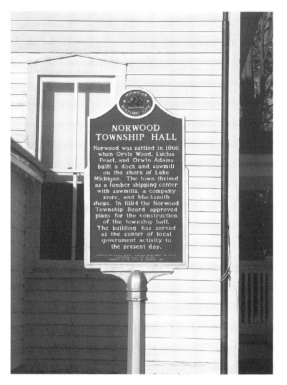

Norwood Township Hall, a Michigan Historic Site

the joy of hunting stones. She said she wanted to do a book someday—I hope she does. This is a very nice spot for a picnic and a good day of rock hunting—enjoy!

Atwood (adorable!)

Again heading south from Charlevoix, *just* north of Atwood take a right on Rex Beach Road off of US 31. It is two miles to the beach and you do pass some interesting

Entering Antrim Creek Natural Area off Rex Beach
Road

The beach at Atwood

looking cutbanks on the way (I stopped on my second trip here and found four really nice stones). Take the road into the Antrim Creek Natural Area. Once you park the car, there is a nice path down the hill to the beach. I found two Petoskeys that weighed about 10 pounds each, about 1/3 actual Petoskey. At the beach itself, there was a lot of algae, but I did find about five good stones in the sandy area. Later that day, my mom and I met a couple at the Weathervane in Charlevoix (what a lunch!) who said they lived in Atwood, just south of the Rex Beach Road. They said they find stones all the time on the beach there as there wasn't much algae. They said their grandchildren found so many, they had to always throw them back after they left. I'll also tell you the view of North and South Fox Islands can be stunning here, so bring the camera and enjoy the rock hunting and the nature preserve.

TORCH LAKE AREA

After 36 years of running rock shops, Betty Dinger knows rocks. Her current store is Dinger's Rock Shop, located by Torch Lake (her slogan is 'ole lady got rocks'). I just had to stop by and see her shop. If it is open when you are near Torch Lake, it is a must for rock enthusiasts. She told me of a place that someone, and this is a direct quote from her, found over 500 rocks in six hours! Now I don't know many people who will hunt Petoskeys for six hours, but extrapolate it down, and it is still a great hunt.

The Nature Preserve across from the Torch Lake Township Park

Now loaded with this information, I went there. It is really quite easy coming from US 31, it is just south of Eastport. Look for Torch Lake Township Day Park. It is about ½ mile to Lake Michigan. I didn't see hundreds—maybe about ten. Bruce was there years earlier and he didn't find as many as I did. Wild goose chase from the cunning rock collector or just the luck of the draw? I say luck of the draw, as that is the case for every place you go, and again, is what makes it fun.

Many think that Torch Lake might be the best inland lake to find Petoskeys. They find a lot of stones at the YMCA camp—Hayo-went-ha—and other places around the lake, especially toward the northern end, which is rockier. If you know someone who has a cottage there, you are in luck. It is also such a magnificent lake, it's just fun to drive around it and enjoy the views.

Rapid City

How do you find a special spot to look for stones? Ask a local. I stopped in to get gas in Kalkaska and asked a couple of the ladies who worked there where they looked for Petoskeys. One lady said her boyfriend finds a lot at the Rapid River in Rapid City. Now it was winter when she told me, so when I went there, I had a hard time getting to the river, and it was really flowing. I guess that is why its called the Rapid River! I didn't find any, but this will be a place that I check on when the snow melts—and I'll have my hip waders to make it easier to get around. I did make are few calls to friends and they said it would make sense that the stones would be there, since it is so close to the Petoskey-rich Torch Lake.

Elk Rapids

I am not sure if I am just overly sentimental or not, but I learned the fun of finding Petoskeys with my mom at the old Kay-n-Ray Resort, 2 miles north of the Lochenheath golf course—this was well before the Grand Traverse Resort was built. My mom and I would find hundreds of them back in the early 1970s, so when I went back in the fall of 2003, looking to see if the old cabins at the resort still existed (they did, but the resort was now a park), my mom, and son and I had to check to find some. It was so windy my eyes were watering, and the rocks had a lot of algae on them, but I found two nice Petoskeys in the dry sand, then it was back to the car to warm up, and when my eyes quit watering, to verify if they really were Petoskeys. They were, and you might have some nice luck here, too. Go north from Traverse City, and two miles north of Lochenheath golf course, take a left at Kay-n-Ray Road and go to the end, which is right at the water. This goes to prove again, find your own spots as they can be cherished memories for many reasons.

North of Eastport

A couple of miles past Eastport, on US 31, begins a wonderful stretch of cutbanks about 30 feet high. They run intermittently for miles. I didn't have all day, but from the success I had in a short time, I suspect this stretch might be loaded.

One of the many cutbanks on US 31 near Eastport

LEELANAU COUNTY

Leelanau State Park, (Northport)

At the end of Densmore Road, off of 629 (by the Woolsey Airport) there is a hiking trail called the Lake Michigan Trail. It is about 1.3 miles to the beach, but it is a very good place to find Petoskeys at Cathead Bay, which is otherwise almost impossible to get to.

Pyramid Point

This has been one of my favorite places for a long time, the views out to the Manitou islands, hundreds of feet above Lake Michigan, are spectacular. The hike to get to

These signs give you three great options for Petoskey stone hunting.

Pyramid Point is one of the many places to look for Petoskeys in the National Lakeshore.

this view is easy enough that my spry 77-year-old mother easily made it up to enjoy the view. Little did I know that you can find Petoskeys here quite easily, many of them the size of baseballs.

There are two problems. The first is the sign saying don't hike down the dune due to erosion problems and the danger it presents—there was a landslide a number of years ago and an entire section of the dune ended up in the water. The second is the hike back up if you do go down.

A few years ago I found a way that eliminated the risk of walking down to the beach, and the nearly impossible task of getting back up. This is the way to go, and I even found two Petoskeys on the walk to the beach.

Here's the back way to the beach. Take 669 to Lake. Take a left on the last road past Shalda Creek Bridge. Take a left at the fork in the road which leads to a circle parking area. Walk about two miles to the base of a dune, then take a right to the lake—you'll hear the waves! Then walk south and you'll be at the base of Pyramid Point, a great place to hunt stones, and as wonderful a walk as there is. Maybe even take a little swim or nap on the beach.

Boulders at Thoreson Road

Going north on M-22 out of Glen Arbor, take a left on Thoreson Road. Go about 9/10 of a mile and take a right on Sunset Drive and go just under ½ of a mile. Then take a right on a road that doesn't have a sign, then take a right at the "T," which is a seasonal road that takes you to a little parking area for a small number of cars. Go down to the beach, which is a very short walk. Then walk north for about 5-10 minutes. The boulders can have a lot of algae on them, so bring a scrub brush to scrub the rocks. You should also bring a pair of water shoes or old shoes because there are a lot of zebra mussels.

You should also bring a camera, because many won't believe you . . . Petoskey boulders.

Christmas Cove

I used to work with this great lady named Amy, who grew up in Traverse City, and when I asked her where her friends would hunt Petoskeys, she immediately replied,

Petoskey stone hunting with kids generates great memories.

The parking area for boulders near Thoreson Road

Looking north from the parking area near Thoreson Road

The beach at Christmas Cove is very close to the parking area.

"Christmas Cove!" So the next time I got near Northport, off I went, kids in tow. We stopped at the gas station in Northport and I asked the owner where it was. He pulled out a map and handed it to me. "I guess you have a few people ask you, right?" He chuckled, and replied back, "Only about a thousand per year!"

Follow M-201 north out of Northport and follow the signs to Christmas Cove. You will take a left on Kilcherman Road which will turn into Christmas Cove Road. Take it right down to the lake.

With that knowledge, I followed the map to Christmas Cove thinking it would surely be picked over. How wrong I was the day we were there. With a five-year-old and an eleven-year-old, we spotted over 50 stones in an hour. I've gone back later, and didn't get that many, but I've always been able to find a few perfect keepers.

You'll also love the town of Northport, a charming village you'll surely enjoy.

Peterson Park

Again, driving north on M-201 out of Northport, you will see the sign for Peterson Park. It will have you veer left which after about 50 yards "Ts" and then you go left on Kitchen Road, which will turn into Peterson Park Road. Take a right into the park, which again is a seasonal road that takes you down to the lake. Once at the park, enjoy the view—it is to die for! After you've soaked in the view, go down the stairs, about a couple hundred feet, to the

The entrance to Peterson Park

View from the playground at Peterson Park

beach. When you get to the bottom of the stairs, you will find the beach covered with big rocks, so you have arrived at a prime location for as far as you can see. You will find nice stones here, and baseball sized ones, too. You might not find as many stones as you can at Christmas Cove, but they will be bigger. Bruce says that the further south you go, the better it gets. A visual reference that he uses is the remains of an old ship wreck. You should also plan in advance for a picnic, because you *will* want to stay longer than just for hunting. There is also a really nice playground for kids.

One more plus to Peterson Park, I have it on good authority that there are boulders here, further out from the shore. Yes, I will put my swim goggles on and check on it when the waters are warm enough. If you try, make sure there are only minimal waves, as the undertow in the big lake can be dangerous.

There is a story, unconfirmed, about the area south of Peterson Park. The story goes like this. A collector had two boys in college who would come home during summer vacation and ask for money. He told the boys that if they wanted money, to come to this stretch of beach and collect stones, for which they would be paid. At one point, he weighed them. That's when he found he had purchased, over many summers, two tons of stones!

Seasonal roads and other side roads

This is certainly a bit vague, but I've given some fairly specific spots so far. So while driving from Northport to Leland, and south again to Glen Arbor (don't forget about Antrim County), there are a lot of roads that you know head toward the lake—is your favorite spot waiting to be found here?

Leland

Just three streets north of Leland, take a left, toward Lake Michigan on North Street and go to the public access. Walk down to the lake and you have arrived at not only one of the most beautiful places to hunt for Petoskeys (the Manitou Islands look like you can touch them), but a

The sign greeting you off of North Street in Leland

Looking north from the beach in Leland

darned good place to find stones. I found fourteen stones right after a storm dumped a ton of sand on the beach, making it tougher to find them, but I felt the place was magic. Now if you will walk the beach far enough to the north, past the point, you will find some really big Petoskeys out in the water.

Whaleback (Petoskey Reef)
South of Leland, turn right at the Marathon station, and it is a short drive to Van's Beach which leads to another public access. Walk down to the beach and go south toward Whaleback Point. It is a brisk fifteen-minute walk. There are boulders the same size as those north of Glen Arbor. It

The entry way to the beach just south of Leland

Looking south to Whaleback from the Leland Beach

The rocky beach at Whaleback

A nice piece of Petoskey embedded in one of the
larger stones south of Leland

was nearly winter when I checked this one out, so I only saw Petoskeys from the beach, but it sure looked the same (see photograph), and my source has family ties back to the early 20s, so she is someone who would know. The good people at Leelanau Books said big ones were down there, too. Trust me, it will be one of the first places I swim when the water warms up so I can see them for myself. If it is anything like Glen Arbor, bring some water shoes so the zebra mussels don't get you.

I stopped at the Whaleback Inn and talked with owner Scott Koehler and he said his son finds stones on the Whaleback Trail and they also find stones in front of their cottages on Lake Leelanau as well. Looks like a nice place to stay.

Lake Leelanau

Bingham's Landing. It used to be called Chap's Landing, as there once stood a party store/gas station run by Mr. Chap. Here are directions from Traverse City. Take M-22 north toward Suttons Bay. Take a left on Cherry Bend Road. The first stop sign is about 3.5 miles. Take a right at the sign, which is County Road 641—this is a gorgeous road to drive. Go north four miles (there's a nice cutbank three miles down) to Bingham Road. The landing is on the left. There is a small public beach. Though the water was really clean, I didn't think I'd find any. I did find three small stones, but you have to believe that Mr. Chap had a lot of Petoskey stones, don't you?

Sleeping Bear Bay

Now I've been here a few times and haven't found a thing, but repeatedly, others have told me they've hit pay dirt there, especially at Sleeping Bear Point where it is rockier, and wind conditions can reveal new treasures. This is another sterling example that you never know what you will or will not find on your journey. I will say the sunsets are as good as any I've seen, so bring your camera.

BENZIE COUNTY AND SOUTH

Point Betsie

One of the most photographed lighthouses in the country. I've found some stones here, more to the north, but I hiked back through the dunes to get there. For me, it wasn't the best place, but the lighthouse and hiking area is worth a visit.

Crystal Lake

There is a water quality researcher near Ann Arbor, Michigan, who shared with me the rumor that there was a Petoskey—thirteen feet in diameter—somewhere near the outlet at Crystal Lake (off Mollineaux Road) I have never heard this rumor, and I've never found a Petoskey at Crystal Lake, but who's to say it doesn't exist?

After a big storm like this one, your chances of finding Petoskeys increase.

Onekama

Bruce has had many customers come into his shop with stories and proof that they've done well in Onekama. They wouldn't tell him where, but it shows that there is a lot of beach south of Point Betsie that is worth exploring. The drive down M-22 has some very scenic vistas, so enjoy and see what back roads to the beach you can find.

MACKINAC ISLAND

Phil Porter, Director of the Mackinac Historic Parks Commission, and a lifelong resident of Mackinac, said that he has never found, nor heard of anyone finding, a Petoskey stone on the island. That said, he quickly added that there are many fossils on the shores and other interesting stones. With the entire island surrounded with stones, even if there aren't Petoskeys, it is a great place to see what you can find, and if you do find a Petoskey, have a witness and get a picture.

UPPER PENINSULA

According to Central Michigan University Associate Professor Kathy Benison, there are Petoskeys in the Upper Peninsula. They are not, however, on the lake shores, but rather in the inland bedrock. Now that's not the best place to find them, but if you are in the UP, don't forget to look.

How to Polish Petoskeys

There are many different levels of polishing Petoskeys. People do it commercially, people do it for hobbies, and of course, it makes a great afternoon project with the kids. This section will give you all three ways to enjoy making your stones shine.

Polishing by hand
Let's start with the best way to start sharing what to do with your freshly found batch of Michigan's state stone. Make it an afternoon project after a mid morning hunt, and maybe a picnic. It is a superb way to top off the perfect day, and your kids will love it, especially on a rainy day.

All you need to get started are the following materials:
220 grit wet or dry sandpaper
600 grit wet or dry sandpaper
Cerium oxide or aluminum oxide (which is found at most rock shops)
Corduroy, felt or silk cloths

1) Take your rough unpolished rock and sand it for 15-30 minutes with the 220 grit sandpaper.
2) Then sand it for 15-30 minutes with the 600 grit sandpaper. Keep the paper moist while sanding.
3) Polish by hand with your moist cloth and the cerium oxide/aluminum oxide for another 30-60 minutes.

Polishing with an arbor
What you need:
Sanding belts
100 grit sandpaper
220 grit sandpaper
600 grit sandpaper
Zam (available at most rock shops)
safety goggles
an arbor to turn the belt and buff

1) Put the 100 grit sandpaper on the arbor and sand the unpolished rock for 2-3 minutes.
2) Put the 220 grit sandpaper on the arbor and sand for 2-3 minutes.
3) Put the 600 grit sandpaper on the arbor and sand for 2-3 minutes.
4) Polish with Zam and buff for 1-2 minutes.
5) * Use safety goggles with the sanding belts and Zam.

Polishing with a rock tumbler
What you need:
3lb or 6 lb rock tumbler
600 grit (silican carbide)
cloth buff and Zam or an arbor or cloth buff and cerium oxide

1) Tumble for 2 days with 600 grit.
2) Cloth buff for 1-2 minutes with an arbor and Zam, or 15–30 minutes with cloth and cerium oxide by hand.

Finger nail polish, lacquer, and polyurethane
These methods will not give the fine polish you will get with the above methods, but they do offer a very quick solution to get a polish, and when time is limited and you still want to see the stones shine, it does work. Do this in a well-ventilated area.

Diamond polishing kit
Barranca Dimond Products makes a polishing unit light enough to move over the surface of large stones that are too heavy to lift easily. Their address is 18205 S. Broadway Street, Gardena, CA 90248, (310) 523-5867. They are also available through some rock shops.

ROCK SHOPS

There are some great rock shops all over Michigan. Make it a point to search them out, because it is here that you will find some beautiful specimens. You will also find Petoskey jewelry and many other unique items that people make with them—mail boxes, small lighthouses. Maybe they will even share a few secret places with you for hunting.

NOTES ON MY PETOSKEY STONE HUNTS

NOTES ON MY PETOSKEY STONE HUNTS

NOTES ON MY PETOSKEY STONE HUNTS

NOTES ON MY PETOSKEY STONE HUNTS

NOTES ON MY PETOSKEY STONE HUNTS

NOTES ON MY PETOSKEY STONE HUNTS

NOTES ON MY PETOSKEY STONE HUNTS

NOTES ON MY PETOSKEY STONE HUNTS